HAVE GOALS NOT GUNS

YOUTH/STUDENT EDITION

WANDA MARTIN

Have Goals Not Guns Youth Edition Action Guide

Copyright © 2022 by Wanda Martin.

All rights reserved. In accordance with the U.S. Copyright Act of 1976, the scanning, uploading, and electronic sharing of any part of this book without permission of the publisher constitute unlawful piracy and theft of the author's intellectual property. If you would like to use material from the book (other than for review purposes), prior written permission must be obtained by contacting the author at info@wandamartin.org.

www.wandamartin.org

ISBN: 978-1-951838-26-3

Published By: 90 Day Legacy Builders
www.90daylegacybuilders.com

ACKNOWLEDGEMENT

I dedicate this book in honor of my niece, Latia Jones who while at the age of 20 and pursuing her GED at Temple University, fell victim to gun violence via some youths on May 14, 2012, while sitting on a porch having a conversation with her friend. Rest well in Heaven, Latia. You're greatly missed.
Aunt Wanda

FROM THE DESK OF MS. JOYCE ABBOTT

As an educator for over 25 years with the School District of Philadelphia, and the namesake of the Emmy Award-winning television series "Abbott Elementary", I know first-hand the importance of goals for youth/students and how impactful they are in their achievement.

Setting goals helps youth/students focus and create a set of achievements for a specific time. Setting goals assist our youth/students with increasing self-confidence, developing work ethic, and building perseverance.

The increase in homicidal violence involving youth has drastically risen. This has affected many families and communities in a devastating way. Having goals brings about new behaviors. Goals can transform a dismal life or situation into a life of purpose. A life of hope. A life of joy.

Wanda is passionate about helping our young people transform their lives through her dedicated work with Goal Setting Strategies. I implore all gatekeepers, educators, politicians, religious leaders, law enforcers, parents/grandparents, family members, and every member of the respective community of a young person to implement these effective strategies.

Collectively, we can help our youth Have Goals, Not Guns and make a difference in their lives, communities, and world.

I salute Wanda for this remarkable work!

Ms. Joyce Abbott
The Real Miss Abbott/Namesake of Abbott Elementary

> Wanda Martin's goal-setting teaching is transformative and not only will improve your mindset, but she also gives you practical tools to stay the course.
> ~Arian Simone
> Serial Entrepreneur, Philanthropist, Angel Investor, Best Selling Author, Featured in Forbes & Essence Magazines

> Wanda's goal setting strategies have the power to not only change life but it will improve your life.
> ~Patty Aubrey,
> CEO of the Jack Canfield Companies, #1 Best Selling author of "Permission Granted"

> Wanda's "Goals Not Guns" concept strategically motivates youth to dream beyond their norms and create a better world for themselves.
> ~Shante' Antrom, Ed.D.
> Executive Director
> Oxford Circle Christian Community Development Association

TESTIMONIALS

MEET YOUR INSTRUCTOR

WANDA MARTIN
Premier Goal Setting Expert, Author, Speaker & TV Host

Wanda Martin is a premier goal-setting expert who specializes in and offers practical tools, tips, and strategies to Elementary, Middle, High School, and College students who are motivated to learn about goals and define them in a way that will create a definitive pathway to success.

With over 15+ years of experience, Wanda has been heralded as one of the nation's leading goal-setting experts. She's assisted students and youth everywhere to discover their purpose, refine their self-image, and illuminate their pathways and dreams toward their own defined success.

This "HAVE GOALS NOT GUNS" comprehensive action guide is sure to offer practical solutions for American communities working with our youth against gun violence.

THE STORY BEHIND...
HAVE GOALS NOT GUNS

On May 14, 2012, my niece Latia Jones, was sitting on the porch talking to her male friend, when a young guy, with a gun, walked up on the porch and shot and killed them both...execution style.

According to the investigations, Latia was an innocent victim and was just at the wrong place at the wrong time. Latia died a few hours later at the hospital.

What most people didn't know about Latia was that at the time of her demise, she was enrolled in Temple University's G.E.D. program, to accomplish her goal of furthering her education and becoming a Forensic Psychologist. Latia had a strong desire to study the behavior of why youths kill other youths due to losing many friends to gun violence.

In memory of Latia, this course was been established to assist with combating the gun violence that's been plaguing the youths in our city, state, and country.

It's my desire that youths will work on and pick up having goals, like my niece Latia did, and if they have a gun, to put it down to produce success in their lives and a brighter future.

STATISTICS BEHIND...
HAVE GOALS NOT GUNS

According to the Gun Violence Archive, so far in 2022, at least 653 children and teens in the U.S. have been killed by guns. Another 1,609 children and teens have been injured by firearms. Guns are now the leading cause of death among young people in the U.S.

According to the Philadelphia Police Department, teenagers and children make up a growing number of gun violence victims and perpetrators, a problem city and school officials have been struggling to address. This year, 96 fatal and nonfatal shooting victims were between the ages of 13-19 and 12 homicide victims were young people under 18. "Gun violence isn't just a school issue," said Armando Ortez, a senior at Northeast High School and a student representative on the Philadelphia Board of Education. "It's a community issue." Carrying a handgun has become significantly more common among teenagers over the last two decades.

In the past two years, community-based youth violence has increased significantly for reasons including disputes that begin or escalate on social media and drug robberies — and many of the incidents involve guns, county officials reported.

To date, The Philadelphia Police Dept. has recovered more than 730 guns since the year began; 110 of the weapons recovered are privately manufactured firearms, known as "ghost guns." Authorities say the amount is set to exceed last year's amount of weapons recovered, which was 1,192.

"We're in a crisis with our kids," County Council member Andrew Friedson (D-District 1) said this week during a youth safety presentation, "I think these challenges are going to get a lot worse before they get a lot better." (The Washington Post-Nicole Asbury).

Welcome to
HAVE GOALS NOT GUNS GOAL SETTING COURSE

Did you know that the University of Scranton did a research and discovered that at the beginning of every year, many individuals set goals but 92% of them never achieve them? This means only 8% of Americans actually achieve the goals they set out to accomplish! This comprehensive goal-setting action guide has been designed to educate you with practical goal-setting strategies and self-discipline techniques to enable you to become a part of the elite number, the 8% ...no matter how young or old you are.

***To receive your free 8% wristband to sport daily and act as a reminder of your goals, visit www.wandamartin.org.

Have Goals Not Guns

» Table of Contents

15	WHY HAVE GOALS	**61**	PRINCIPLE #5
31	PRINCIPLE #1	**65**	PRINCIPLE #6
35	PRINCIPLE #2	**71**	PRINCIPLE #7
43	PRINCIPLE #3	**75**	PRINCIPLE #8
51	PRINCIPLE #4	**78**	ANSWERS

Youth Edition

There has never been and never will be a better time to start designing your future than now.

"Age is an issue of mind over matter. If you don't mind, it doesn't matter."
~ Mark Twain

One of the things I stress to youths/students of today is that you're never too young to have goals and it's never too late to be great. In other words, DON'T LET YOUR AGE DEFINE OR STOP YOU.

The reason why I'm encouraging you not to let your age define you is because sometimes young people see their age as a major wall when talking or dreaming about achieving a big goal or being successful. In my opinion, your age doesn't matter at all and therefore, you can be young and already have the mindset to be a successful person.

No matter if your age is 2, 12, or 22, if you think you have it in you to do something big, then go ahead and give it one hundred percent and follow your dreams. Success will come. If you don't believe me, here are a couple of examples that illustrate better what I mean:

Examples:

The 44th President said he knew he wanted to be President of the United States of America when he was in grade school.

BARACK OBAMA

The richest man in the world knew he wanted to be a rich business man when he was just a youth.

BILL GATES

Oprah Winfrey knew she wanted to be an actress when she was just a kid.

OPRAH WINFREY

DON'T THINK SMALL... DREAM BIG

When Philadelphia Phillies pitcher Tug Mcgraw-father of legendary country singer Tim Mcgraw- struck out batter, Willie Wilson to help the Phillies win the 1980 World Series Title, he was asked about the experience on the mound that day. Tim's response was this, "It was as if I'd been there a thousand times before." When I was growing up, I would pitch to my father in the backyard. We would always get to where it was the bottom of the ninth in the World Series with two outs and three men on base. I would always bear down and strike them out."

Because Tug has conditioned his mind day after day in his backyard not to think small but to believe big, the day to achieve his goal eventually arrived when he was living this dream as a reality.

Don't cheat yourself out of living your dreams and achieving *BIG GOALS* by thinking too small in life. If you believe big and do the work, your dreams too can become a reality.

WHAT ARE YOUR GOALS AND DREAMS...
Reflection Page

LET'S DREAM...

I want you to write down all the dreams, desires, or goals you've ever had while growing up. While thinking about the things you've always wanted to do, be, or have, don't limit yourself by being practical or realistic (some would say). Limiting yourself will limit your potential and we don't want that to happen so just...GO FOR IT.

_____
_____
_____
_____
_____
_____
_____
_____
_____
_____

> Each of us has a fire in our hearts for something. It's our goal to find it and keep it.
>
> MARYLOU RETTON
> AMERICAN FIRST FEMALE GYMNAST TO WIN THE OLYMPIC ALL-AROUND ATHLETE" TITLE.

WHY HAVE GOALS?

"You don't have to be great to get started, but you do have to get started to be great."
Lee J. Colan

Have you ever wondered why some youths/students are so good at fulfilling their dreams, breaking records in their sporting events, succeeding academically in all their classes and living a life of purpose? What is their "secret sauce" for success or becoming the best version of themselves? For me, I used to always ask myself this question while watching TV of young actors playing their roles successfully in movies or observing amazing youths break records in sporting events or during graduation, watching how they would receive Honor Roll Awards, accolades, or the highest achievements in the school.

Some people would say that all you need to do is work hard to achieve what you want in life. Others would say that these "special" youths/students were born with access and/or a silver spoon in their mouths in order to receive the best education or the best coaches in life. But the truth is, according to statistics, those who create goals (youths or adults) and develop amazing self-discipline habits are more likely to come out on top and achieve their life's dreams or goals, while others sit on the sideline wishing they could.

As a youth, having goals are necessary and something you will need to apply for the rest of your life. Having goals will serve many purposes pulling you forward, and acting as a guide for the choices you make now and in the future. In other words, when you have goals, they will act as your own personal tour guide that you can follow as you make choices about classes, athletic activities, relationships, educational interests, college, and your future. Let's discover other reasons why it's important to have goals because all successful students rose to success because they began with a set of goals.

LET'S DISCUSS WHY HAVE GOALS?

Having goals is essential to being successful and here's why:

- They provide <u>Directions</u>.

- They help build <u>Confidence</u>.

- They give you something to <u>Work Towards</u>.

- They keep you from <u>Limiting Yourself</u>.

- They help you to achieve <u>More</u>.

- They keep you <u>Motivated</u>.

- They increase your <u>Bank Account</u>.

- They help you to become <u>Successful</u> in life.

***Now let's review each of them in more detail.

GOALS PROVIDE DIRECTIONS

Most youths/students are always seeking direction for their lives such as what school or classes to attend the following year, what business can they start to make money, what sporting team should they join that will give them an advantage in life, or what friends should they connect with, but when you have goals, it will provide you the direction that you are looking for to get you ahead in the classroom, in your sporting game and in life.

Having goals is like having a GPS in your car, they have a way of taking you directly to your destination.

Without goals, your life as a student will be like a cruise ship with no captain steering it. Your life will just drift along without any meaning or purpose. When you have goals, your life will be like a speedboat that can take you directly to where you want to go with great speed.

As a student, if you want to arrive at your:
- Dream School
- Dream Business
- Dream Success
- Dream Desire

with great speed, having goals will make that happen for you.

GOALS HELP BUILD CONFIDENCE

Low self-esteem and a lack of confidence are some of the reasons why some students are generally scared to move out of their comfort zone to set goals. However, you will find that when you start setting goals and accomplishing them, you will see how it has a way of boosting your confidence.

Having goals can boost your confidence to:
- Get all A's
- Write that book or song
- Start that business
- Apply for that job
- Lose weight
- Become a scholar athlete
- Ask that girl or guy out
- Etc.

Whatever goal you have been lacking the confidence to accomplish, setting goals will boost your confidence to accomplish it.

Brian Tracy made this statement, "When you commit to one sound goal and you achieve it, you build confidence within yourself that says, you got this."

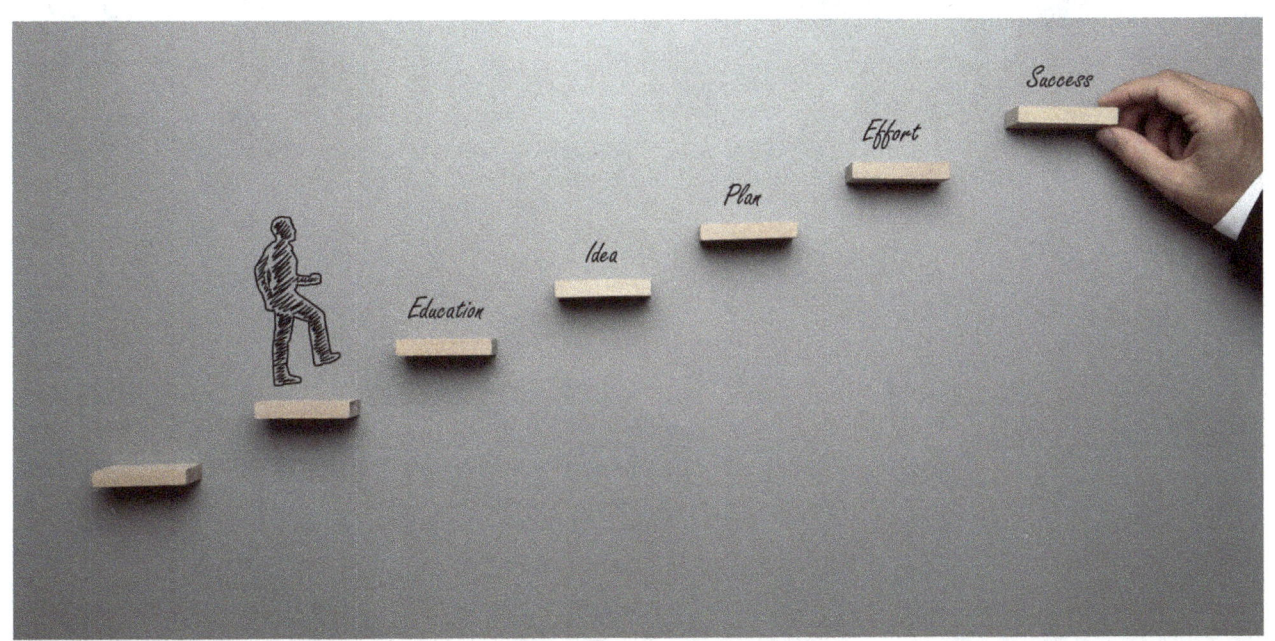

GOALS GIVE YOU SOMETHING TO WORK TOWARDS

Students who are bored with life, school, and at home are the ones who don't have any goals that they are working towards. If you are bored or unhappy with life or even school, could it be that you don't have any significant goals you are working towards to motivate you?

Setting goals can be very effective in increasing motivation to work towards something significant. I've seen tremendous changes in people's attitudes, even students when they became motivated to work towards a goal.

For example, my son Tony Martin, 16 years of age, set a goal to become the only freshman to make his school's varsity Basketball team, and therefore he would wake up at 6 am to work out and do shoot around, run several miles in the hot sun during the summer months and also put his body through intense pressure by lifting weights seven days a week. As a result of his hard work and dedication to this goal, not only did he make the varsity team, he has earned a spot as a starter, meaning he is one of the top players in the starting lineup at Christopher Dock Mennonite School.

GOALS KEEP YOU FROM LIMITING YOURSELF

Have you heard the story about the AFRICAN IMPALA? If not, this is what you should know. They can jump almost 10 feet high and 30 feet long yet, you will find them in a zoo behind a 4-foot wall.

- Why?
    - The African Impala will not attempt to jump where he can't see first. So since he cannot see over the 4-foot wall around him, he just stays trapped year after year in that small area.

As a student, if you don't set goals you will limit yourself and not be able to see where you are going and therefore will stay trapped and won't be able to reach your greatest potential or go far in life.

In order to reach your goals and dreams, you need to push through your limits and past your comfort zone. There are no shortcuts.

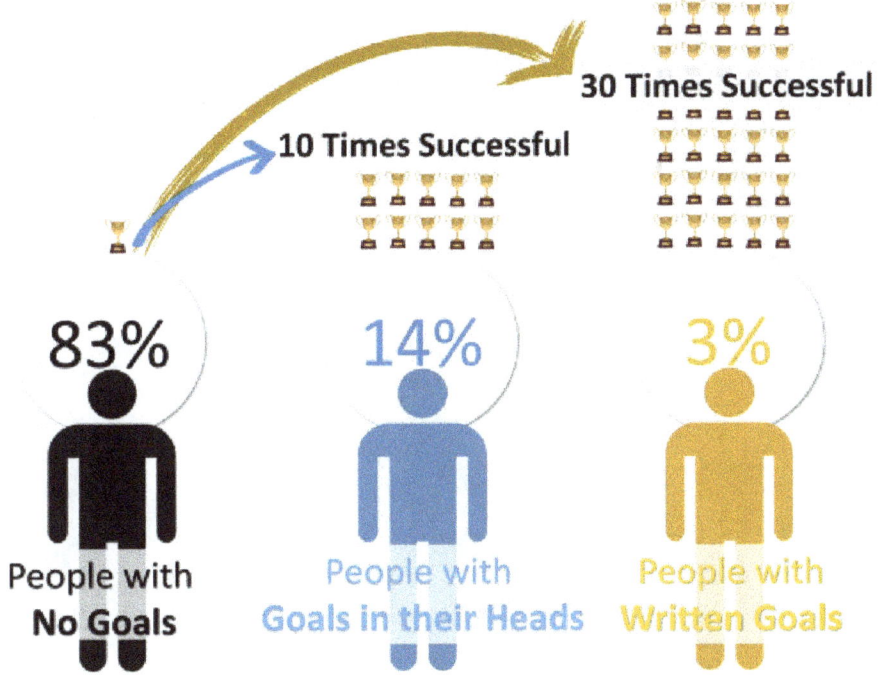

GOALS HELP YOU TO ACHIEVE MORE

Professor David Kohls from Virginia Tech did a research about students and goals. One day he asked the students on campus, "How many of you have goals?"

- 83% had absolutely no goals
- 14% had goals but never wrote them down
- 3% had goals and wrote them down

Notice from the graphic above, the 2nd and 3rd groups were more successful (or achieved more) than the first group... which didn't have any goals at all.

In addition, when Professor Kohl followed the 3% of students after ten years, they made more money than the rest and all became millionaires. Students with goals earn more and actually achieve MORE!

GOALS KEEP YOU FEELING HAPPY

Having goals can help make you happier and feel good on purpose. Seriously, it can. You see, when students write down their goals and commit to going after something bigger and better than what they have at the moment, they create hope and happiness for themselves. Hope and happiness for a better tomorrow, hope and happiness for a better future, and hope and happiness that their goals will be achieved.

Whenever you achieve your goals in any way, whether it's passing your most challenging exam of the semester, or being the best athlete in the game, you are going to feel good about them naturally. This good feeling comes from your brain that releases a neurotransmitter called dopamine that motivates you to feel good and to go after another goal.

Having clearly defined goals will help you feel good about yourself in more ways than none. Even while reading this action guide, you probably are feeling good right now because you are being educated and motivated to go after your goals.

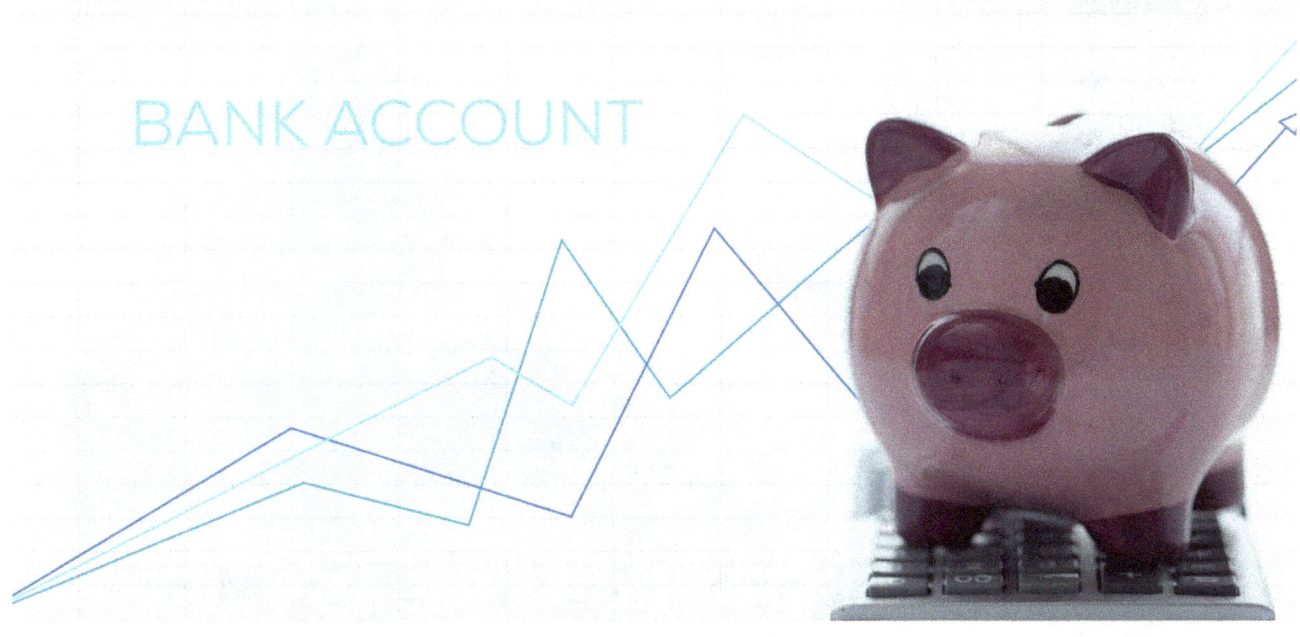

GOALS INCREASE BANK ACCOUNTS

Learning how to set goals will drastically increase your bank balance. Goal-setting author, Jim Rohn, stated that people (students) without goals have less than $200 in their bank accounts.

In the beginning, I had a hard time believing this statement, so I began asking individuals with no goals, did Jim Rohn's statement rings to be true in their lives, and almost everyone I asked said, "Yes." However, after learning to set goals, they opened a bank account, if they didn't already have one, and observed that their bank accounts changed for the better.

As for me, goal setting has drastically increased my bank account and will do the same for you as a youth or student when you learn how to set and achieve goals properly.

GOALS ARE ESSENTIAL TO BECOMING SUCCESSFUL.

There are no highly successful people (youths) who became successful without having goals and a good example of this can be found in the life of BRIAN SCUDAMORE (1-800-GOT-JUNK).

It was said that in 1989 while waiting in line at a McDonald's drive-thru, he observed a beat-up old pickup truck advertising their junk removal service. Brian thought to himself, "I can do better than that." Shortly thereafter, Brian invested $1000 in the venture—$700 for a pickup truck and the rest for fliers and business cards. Brian worked on his business and goal to be successful, and by the eighth year, his business made one million dollars in revenue. Brian SCUDAMORE became a success because he made having a goal essential for his life, and he went after it.

Ryan Khaji (10 yrs old), a successful YOUTUBER over Ryan's World, has over 20 million subscribers and 9 YOUTUBE channels. Last year, Ryan made over 30 million dollars and was able to become successful as a student and youth because he had...GOALS.

WHY HAVE GOALS MULTIPLE CHOICE QUIZ

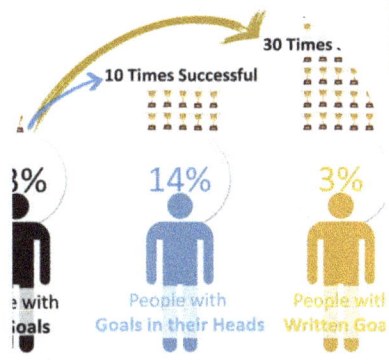

ACCORDING TO PROFESSOR DAVID KHOLS, PEOPLE WITH GOALS...

A. WASTE TIME

B. PROCRASTINATE

C. ACHIEVE MORE

D. GO TO COLLEGE

LIKE THE AFRICAN IMPALA, IF YOU CAN'T SEE WHERE YOU ARE GOING, YOU WILL:

A. LIMIT YOURSELF

B. DOUBT YOURSELF

C. MISS YOUR GOAL TARGET

HAVING GOALS WILL :

A. INCREASE YOUR BANK ACCOUNT

B. HELP YOU TO BECOME SUCCESSFUL

C. KEEP YOU FEELING HAPPY

D. ALL OF THE ABOVE

The trouble with not having a goal is that you can spend your entire life running up and down the field and never score.

YOU MUST HAVE GOALS!

ACTION ITEM

WHY SHOULD YOU HAVE GOALS?

IN THE SPACES BELOW, WRITE DOWN ALL THE REASONS WHY YOU PERSONALLY BELIEVE IT'S IMPORTANT FOR *YOU* TO HAVE GOALS.

- [ ] Ex.- Having Goals will keep me focused.
- [ ]
- [ ]
- [ ]
- [ ]
- [ ]
- [ ]
- [ ]
- [ ]

Those who don't set goals in life end up being controlled and working for those who do.

PAUL SLOANE

THE TOP (8) GOAL SETTING PRINCIPLES EVERY YOUTH/STUDENT SHOULD KNOW....

SETTING GOALS ARE ESSENTIAL.

According to the University of Scranton, a whopping 92% of individuals, which includes youths/students, who set goals, never achieve them which means only 8% do. If you desire to become a part of this elite number, the 8%, then I challenge you to read each Goal Setting principle, take every short quiz, and complete every ACTION ITEM. If you take your time to thoroughly complete every section of this action guide, you will receive some amazing results and will eventually become a part of the 8% club.

The 8% of youths/students who achieve their goals made the following principles a part of their daily routine.

Let's look at these (8) PRINCIPLES.

PRINCIPLE 1:

Have a clear understanding of what Goals are.

What Are Goals?

Goals are things (targets) you want to accomplish or achieve but with a deadline date attached to them. Statistics have said that the average person makes the same goals every year but never achieves them because they have no deadline dates attached to their targets.

Goals are simply dreams with a deadline date. Without a deadline date, a list of goals is just a wish list. In order for something to be described as a goal, it must have a deadline date. *NEVER FORGET THIS!*

EXAMPLES

This is <u>A</u> goal:
- I will learn to play an instrument by the end of the summer.

This is <u>NOT</u> a goal:
  - I will learn how to play an instrument.
    - (Why Not? It has NO deadline date.)

This is <u>A</u> goal:
- I will learn to drive and get my license by December 31st.

This is <u>NOT</u> a goal:
  - I will get my license.
    - (Why Not? It has NO deadline date.)

PRINCIPLE #1 MULTIPLE CHOICE QUIZ

A GOAL IS A TARGET YOU WANT TO ACCOMPLISH BUT WITH A...

A. BEGIN DATE
B. BIRTH DATE
C. DEADLINE DATE
D. WEEKLY DATE

THIS IS A GOAL- I WILL READ FIVE BOOKS THIS YEAR BY MARCH 15TH.

A. TRUE
B. FALSE

THIS IS NOT A GOAL- I WILL LOSE 10 POUNDS BY THE END OF THE YEAR.

A. TRUE
B. FALSE

Write It Down

GOALS

Have fun. Write down some goals you would like to achieve this year with deadlines attached to them.

PRINCIPLE 2:

Carefully Select Your Goals

Goals are targets, and having a target is vital to your success. Without a target, there's nowhere to aim. As a youth/student, you should have a goal/target for your education, faith, fitness, family, future, and friendships because when the target is clear, the results will appear.

What <u>SPECIFIC</u> goals would you like to achieve or accomplish over the next 12 months? This is an important question you need to ask yourself to get started on setting and achieving goals for your life.

How to Select My Goals?

To assist you with selecting your goals, try this task that I've been doing for years.

Brian Tracy, a famous goal-setting author says one of his favorite exercises is to imagine it is December 31st and say, "This has been the most amazing year of my life!" For this statement to be true, what would you like to see happen this year to make this statement true? (Give this some serious thought.) Once you have your answers, write down no more than ten items, and let this become your goal list for the year.

Oh My Gosh! This was my most amazing year!

For this to be the most amazing year of your life, what happened in these areas below?

FITNESS/HEALTH:
- Did you lose weight? How much and By when?
- Did you work out? How often?

FINANCE:
- Did you save or put money away? How much and By when?

FAMILY/FRIENDSHIP:
- Did you spend more time talking to your mom/dad/daily? For how long? How often?
- Did you make new friends this year? How many and By When?

EDUCATION:
- Did you bring your Math/English/History Etc. up a grade? To what grade and by when?
- Did you study for one hour daily?

PRINCIPLE #2 MULTIPLE CHOICE
QUIZ

YOU SHOULD HAVE GOALS SELECTED FOR MULTIPLE AREAS OF YOUR LIFE.

A. TRUE

B. FALSE

YOU SHOULD IMAGINE ABOUT TEN (10) GOALS TO WORK ON THROUGHOUT A YEAR.

A TRUE

B FALSE

WHAT SPECIFIC GOAL WOULD YOU LIKE TO ACHIEVE OR ACCOMPLISH OVER THE NEXT 12 MONTHS?

A. THIS QUESTION IS WHAT I SHOULD <u>NOT</u> ASK MYSELF EVERY YEAR.

B. THIS QUESTION IS WHAT I <u>SHOULD</u> ASK MYSELF EVERY YEAR.

ACTION ITEM

What would you like to see happen by December 31st? What would make this the best year of your life in the areas listed below? **Write down 1-2 goals in each category.** (*Don't forget your deadline date.*)

1. EDUCATION - Receive 90+ in English by June 15th.

2. FINANCE - Save $50 a month by December 31st.

3. FITNESS & HEALTH - Work out 3x a week every month.

4. FAMILY OR FRIENDSHIPS - Talk to my mother daily.

5 FAITH - Pray or read a devotion for 15-20 min. daily.

WRITE IT DOWN. WRITTEN GOALS HAVE A WAY OF CHANGING WISHES INTO WANTS; CAN'TS INTO CANS; DREAMS INTO PLANS; AND PLANS INTO REALITY.
DON'T JUST THINK IT – INK IT!

MICHAEL KORDA

YOUTHS WHO REGULARY WRITE DOWN THEIR GOALS EARN 9 TIMES AS MUCH OVER THEIR LIFETIMES AS THOSE WHO DON'T.

PRINCIPLE 3:

Write Goals Down

Most successful youth/students today have this one thing in common. They write down their goals.

It's not enough to have goals in your head; you must put them in writing as well. *(Don't Think It-Ink It!)*

It has been said that 97% of today's youths are trying to live their lives without any clear written goals. They're missing out on experiencing great success in the classrooms, out on the field/on the court, and in their personal lives. Author Brain Tracy compares not having clearly written goals to "traveling to another city or state without a road map." You may get somewhere eventually, but it will take you much longer to get there because you have nothing written down. Make sure you write down your goals because what's not on paper, will become VAPOR *(disappear)*.

WHY WRITING GOALS DOWN IS A POWERFUL PRACTICE?

This is significant because if you just think about your goals, you are only using the right side of your brain, which is your imaginative center. But if you think about something that you desire or a specific goal, and then write it down, you also tap into the power of your logic-based left side and you send your entire brain and every cell of your body a signal that says, "I want this and I mean it!"

To achieve your goals, you need to get both sides of your brain involved in the process and that comes from not just thinking about them but also writing them down.

When you don't take the time to write down your goals, what you are communicating to your brain is that they are not important enough to write them down. But when your goals are important enough, you will take the time to write them down. Here's a good example with Caleb Maddix.

Caleb Maddix wrote his goals down

This habit of writing down your goals can work for anyone, no matter their age. For example: As a young kid, Caleb Maddix started reading success books at six years old by his father's recommendation. By the age of eight, Caleb's dad had him writing down his goals. They included:

- I will speak with Gary Vaynerchuk. (An Entrepreneur, Author, and Internet personality)
- I will do a Ted talk. (Short talks that present a great idea)
- I will do an event with millionaire, Tony Robbins. (An American Author, Coach, and Speaker)
- I will make $100k by the time I am at the age of 14.
- I will have 100k followers on Facebook.

Everything Caleb wrote down actually happened. Isn't that amazing? Goals work... no matter your age!

***I challenge you to write down 101 goals and watch what will happen as a result of it.

BENEFITS OF WRITING GOALS DOWN:

- Can increase your chance of achieving them by 42%.
    - When you write down your goals, you increase the odds of achieving them greatly.
- Clarifies what you really want.
    - The act of writing your goals down requires a level of clarity that just thinking about them doesn't.
- Makes them real.
    - When you place your goals on a piece of paper, it starts to become more real to you.
- Helps you to stay focused and avoid distractions.
    - When you write your goals down, your desire to achieve those goals gets focused.
- Puts your future in motion.
    - When you write your goals down, it puts them in the atmosphere and causes things to go to work on your behalf and in your life.

Write goals down in the present tense

THIS IS IMPORTANT TO REMEMBER: When you begin to write down your goals, make sure they are in the present tense- because your subconscious mind only understands... NOW.

With that in mind, here is an example to follow when writing down your goal. "I am so happy and grateful now that I am improving my math grade from a B to an A by June 15th at midnight."

Do you see how I ended this statement with a goal in the present tense? Now you try it...

  I am so happy and grateful now that I am _____
  (by when?)_____.

**** Be sure that all of your action words end in (ing).

The action verb ending with -ing will add power to the goals by creating an image of you doing it or experiencing it right now.

By writing your goals down this way, you will create a personal ownership each time you read your goals aloud and it starts to feel more and more real and believable to you. The more you believe in your goal, the more action steps you'll take to turn that goal into reality.

PRINCIPLE #3 MULTIPLE CHOICE QUIZ

ALL GOALS SHOULD BE WRITTEN DOWN IN THE _____ TENSE.

A. PAST

B. PRESENT

WRITING DOWN YOUR GOALS INCREASES YOUR CHANCES BY __.

A. 50%

B. 100%

C. 42%

WHEN YOUR GOALS ARE NOT ON PAPER, THEY WILL BECOME

A. VAPOR (DISAPPEAR)

B. A REALITY

C. UNREACHABLE

ACTION ITEM

21 DAYS WRITING ASSIGNMENT:

1. **WRITE DOWN YOUR GOALS ONCE A DAY**

2. **MAKE SURE YOU WRITE GOALS DOWN IN PRESENT TENSE**

3. **SIT BACK AND WATCH WHAT HAPPENS AFTER 21 DAYS**

Your goals will be so attached to your subconscious mind that you will:

~Remember them with ease.

~Become determined to achieve them.

~Set those goals in motion.

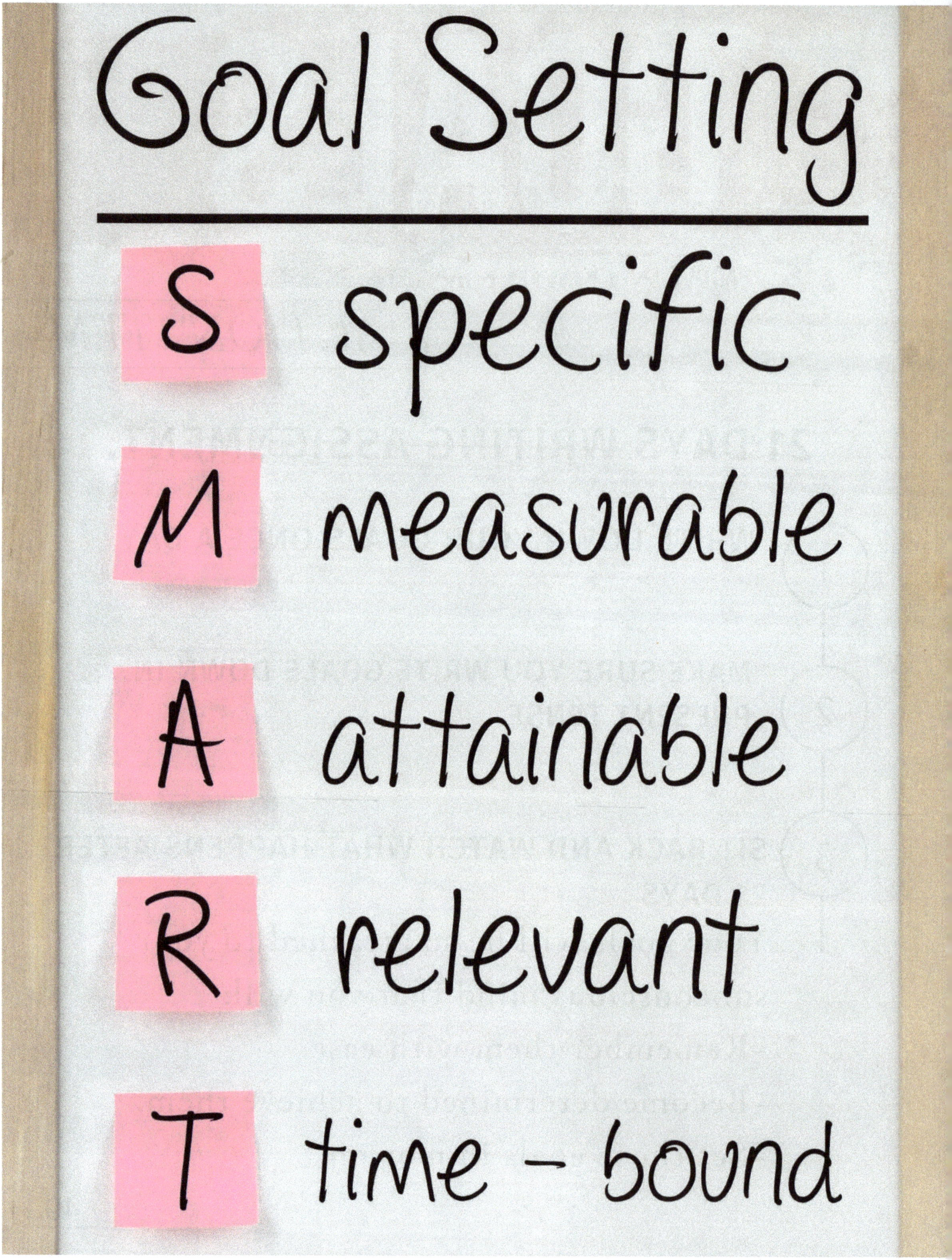

Goal Setting

- **S** specific
- **M** measurable
- **A** attainable
- **R** relevant
- **T** time - bound

PRINCIPLE 4:

MAKE GOALS S.M.A.R.T.

If you desire your goals to work for you and want to increase your chances of success as a youth/student, make sure they are all S.M.A.R.T.

S = SPECIFIC

M = MEASURABLE

A = ACTIONABLE

R = REALISTIC

T = TIMEBOUND

There are many youths today that are missing out on achieving their academic, sports, and/or relationship goals because they fail to make them S.M.A.R.T.

To have S.M.A.R.T. goals will benefit you tremendously as a youth/student both in school, in the workforce and personally and to give you the advantage in these areas, I have provided for you in practical terms and language, what each letter means and how you can apply them to your life in order to make it successful.

S. M. A. R. T.

SPECIFIC:

When it comes to goal setting, you want to be as specific and detailed as possible about exactly what you want to have, be, or do. When your goals are specific, statistics have said that you can achieve them ten times faster all because they are SPECIFIC.

- It's like going to the Mall with your friends. When you know specifically what you want, you can get in and get out. When you don't know specifically what you want, you will remain in the Mall longer than expected, going from store to store because you are not specific about what you want.

When your goals are SPECIFIC, that is when you will get them. When your goals are not specific, the chances of achieving them are slim to none.

- **NOT SPECIFIC**
  - "I will get good grades."
- **SPECIFIC**
  - "I will pass my English class with a 90+ better by June 15th, midnight."

Do you see the difference between a SPECIFIC goal and a NON-SPECIFIC goal? When your goals are specific, they are much more empowering because they are super clear about what needs to be done and when it needs to be done by.

HOW TO MAKE YOUR GOALS SPECIFIC?

To make your goals specific, make sure you have details. The more details you have, the more specific your goals will become. To create goals with details, make sure you can answer these questions:

- *WHAT IS THE GOAL I WANT TO ACCOMPLISH?*
  - I will score ten points a game by the end of the season on November 15th.
- *WHY AM I DOING THIS?*
  - I want to be nominated for my team's MVP.
- *HOW AM I GOING TO GET THIS DONE?*
  - Staying an extra hour after practice daily
- *WHEN WILL I DO THIS?*
  - By November 15TH.

NOTE: By answering these four simple questions, it will help you to make your goals as specific and detailed as possible and help you to achieve them 10 times faster.

S. *M.* A. R. T.

MEASURABLE:

All goals must be measurable (in quantities such as dollars, pages, pounds points, etc.) You need to know when you want them to happen. When there's no criteria for measurement, it's not a goal, it's just something you want, wish, or prefer...it's really just a "good idea." Think about it, how will you know you've reached your goals unless you can measure them?

To have measurable goals, answer the questions "How much?" and "By When?"

Here is a good example:

"I want to lose 10 pounds by May 31st, midnight.
- How much? 10 pounds?
- By when? May 31st at midnight?

As you can see, this example is a clear measurable goal because anybody (such as your friend, parents, coach, etc.) can show up at midnight on May 31st and have you get on a scale to see if you lost 10 pounds or not.

Having measurable goals will enable you to evaluate your progress to see if you have reached it.

Dream Big | Set Goal | Take Action

S. M. A. R. T.

ACTIONABLE:

Every goal should start with an action verb such as quit, run, finish, or start. Inserting an action verb at the beginning of every goal will motivate you to take action.

A Bad example: I want to be more consistent in working out.

A Good example: Start working out 2-3 times a week.

One way to turn your goals into action is to eliminate the phrase "to be" such as in the sentence "I want to be rich." The phrase "to be" is not an action verb. Using the phrase "to be" will prevent you from having clear directions, so stay away from using "to be" phrases and start every goal with an action verb.

S. M. A. R. T.

REALISTIC:

The root word of realistic is real. A realistic goal is something you can do and act on right now in your present reality (IN YOUR SEASON). When you examine your goals carefully to make sure each goal is realistically achievable, you increase your chances for success. Whether at school, home or on the field/court. Setting realistic goals means breaking your big goals down into smaller, more manageable pieces.

EXAMPLE:

| "READ FOUR (4) BOOKS BY DECEMBER 31ST." | **BREAKS DOWN INTO** | READ ONE (1) BOOK EVERY THREE MONTHS |

Don't set all your goals too high because if you do, you will be disappointed when you don't reach them. Set goals that will stretch you and make you grow, but are also attainable.

TIMEBOUND

Every goal needs a deadline date associated with it. If it doesn't have a date, it's not a goal. Most youth/students don't like deadline dates because it brings on pressure but pressure can be a healthy thing. Having a deadline is also essential to achieving your goals and here's why:

- It motivates you and creates a sense of urgency.
    - Ex - When your English teacher gives you an English essay with a due date, that deadline date motivates, creates a sense of urgency, and gets you moving to start working on that assignment.
    - If you have a goal to create a YouTube video or write one blog once a week, that deadline date will create an urgency to complete it.
- It focuses your attention and makes you work towards it.
    - Ex - If you have a Math assignment due on Friday and today is Wednesday; you would want to focus all your attention on that assignment first before you do anything else because of its... deadline date.
- It balances your workload.
    - Meaning deadline dates help you to prioritize tasks, assignments, and activities.
    - Deadlines will help you to spread things out.

<u>WHAT IF YOU MISS YOUR DEADLINE DATE?</u>

If you ever miss making your deadline date, don't panic. It's like if you have to miss a doctor's appointment or a hair dresser/barber appointment; just set a new date. NO BIG DEAL!

Try to understand that life happens to all of us, even you as a youth, and sometimes things come up and get in the way, therefore, it is sometimes necessary to set a new date.

PRINCIPLE #4 MULTIPLE CHOICE QUIZ

HOW MUCH AND BY WHEN FALLS- UNDER WHAT LETTER?

A. S= SPECIFC
B. M= MEASURABLE
C. A= ACTIONABLE
D. T= TIMEBOUND

START ALL GOALS WITH AN ACTION WORDS FALLS UNDER WHAT LETTER?

A. S=SPECIFIC
B. A=ACTIONABLE
C. R= REALISTIC
D. M=MEASURABLE

WHEN YOUR GOALS ARE CLEAR, THE RESULTS WILL APPEAR -FALLS UNDER WHAT LETTER

A. S=SPECIFIC
B. M=MEASURABLE
C. T=TIMEBOUND
D. ALL OF THE ABOVE

A DEADLINE DATE WILL MAKE YOU WORK HARD TOWARDS A GOAL -FALLS UNDER WHAT LETTER?

A. S= SPECFIC
B. T=TIMEBOUND
C. A=ACTIONABLE
D. M=MEASURABLE

ACTION ITEM

LET'S TAKE ONE GOAL YOU WOULD LIKE TO ACHIEVE OVER THE NEXT 12 MONTHS AND MAKE IT S.M.A.R.T.

S	**SPECIFIC** WHAT DO I WANT TO ACCOMPLISH? GIVE AS MANY DETAILS AS POSSIBLE.	
M	**MEASURABLE** HOW WILL I KNOW WHEN IT IS ACCOMPLISHED? HOW MUCH? BY WHEN?	
A	**ACHIEVABLE** START THIS GOAL WITH AN ACTION WORD	
R	**REALISTIC** DOES THIS GOAL SEEM REALISTIC? DO YOU NEED TO BREAK IT DOWN TO A SMALLER GOAL?	
T	**TIME BOUND** WHEN CAN I ACCOMPLISH THIS GOAL? WHAT'S YOUR DEADLINE DATE?	

***Do this exercise for all of your goals.

"If your goal isn't scary and exciting, then it's not a big enough goal for you."

PRINCIPLE 5:
MAKE GOALS EXCITING

All of your goals should be things that excite and motivate you. If you are not excited about your goal, then you will not work hard to achieve it.

With goal setting, you must consistently ask yourself, "Why do I want to accomplish this goal?" Your answer to this question will determine whether or not you are excited about this goal.

REMEMBER THIS: Your goals should be something that you "WANT" to do and not something other people, like your friends, family, teacher, or society "THINK" you should do. This is important for you to know because many adults today who are doctors, lawyers, singers, actors, etc., are not as good as they can be because they did not pursue their own goals that excited them but instead allowed other people to choose and set their goals for them.

Don't let this be you. Figure out the goals you are excited about achieving, why you are excited about achieving them, and make those the goals you set out to pursue.

PRINCIPLE #5 MULTIPLE CHOICE QUIZ

YOUR GOALS SHOULD _____ AND _____ YOU.

A. MOVE AND SHAKE
B. EXCITE AND MOTIVATE
C. INSPIRE AND EXPIRE
D. INFORM AND BUILD

YOUR GOALS SHOULD BE SOMETHING THAT YOU WANT TO DO.

A. TRUE
B. FALSE

IF YOU ARE NOT EXCITED ABOUT YOUR GOALS, THEN YOU WILL NOT WORK HARD TO ACHIEVE THEM.

A. TRUE
B. FALSE

IF A GOAL IS WORTH HAVING, IT'S WORTH BLOCKING OUT SOME TIME DURING YOUR DAY TO REIVEW IT.

PRINCIPLE 6:
REVIEW THEM DAILY

Did you know that the #1 reason why many youths/students today don't achieve their goals is due to not reviewing them? Why take the time to set and write your goals but never go back to review them? If you are going to put forth that kind of effort with your goals, you should go the rest of the way by reviewing them...daily or weekly.

Reviewing goals daily will help you to avoid procrastination and motivate you to achieve them. This process will be a constant reminder of what you need to do. It will continuously pull you forward to reach them.

Trust me, the saying "Out of sight, Out of mind" is a very true statement and when you don't review or look at your goals daily, they will fall out of your mind and eventually out of your life.

When you review your goals every day, read them aloud and make sure you also take the time to visualize yourself achieving them...this is a very important process to seeing them come to pass.

A few suggestions on how you can review your goals daily is by keeping them in a journal, placing them on a 3x5 card to keep with you at all times, place them somewhere in your cell phone or hang on your wall to keep them before your eyes. You may be wondering why taking these extra steps to review your goals are so important the answer is because your brain is constantly processing what's in front of your eyes and this makes it easier for you to act on it.

BENEFITS TO REVIEWING GOALS DAILY

1. <u>YOU BECOME HIGHLY FOCUSED</u>

Most young people are not 100% focused on their goals and are easily distracted therefore, they find it very hard to achieve them.

Reviewing your goals keeps them at the forefront of your mind, which enables you to remain FOCUSED.

2. <u>YOU STRENGTHEN YOUR COMMITMENT TO THEM</u>

When you review your goals every day, it helps you to stay committed to them.

The late Vince Lombardi, a famous football coach said, "Most people fail to stick to their goals not because of lack of desire but due to lack of commitment." It's not enough to be motivated to go after your goals, you also have to be committed.

3. <u>YOU AVOID PROCRASTINATION</u>

Procrastination is one of the greatest enemies of goal achievement and, to guard against it, you should have a daily routine or habit of reviewing your goals consistently!

PRINCPLE #6 MULTIPLE CHOICE QUIZ

HOW OFTEN SHOULD YOU REVIEW YOUR GOALS TO ACHIEVE THEM?

A. WEEKLY

B. MONTHLY

C. DAILY

REVIEWING YOUR GOALS DAILY WILL HELP YOU TO AVOID PROCRASTINATION.

A. TRUE

B. FALSE

WHEN YOU ARE REVIEWING YOUR GOALS, YOU SHOULD ALSO _____ YOURSELF ACHIEVING THEM.

A. WORK

B. REMIND

C. VISUALIZE

D. ALL THE ABOVE

ACTION ITEM:
SELECT WHERE YOU WILL KEEP YOUR GOALS POSTED TO REVIEW DAILY

- ON MY WALL

- IN A FRAME

- IN A BOOK

- ON MY PHONE

- ON MY DESK

YOU CAN'T SOAR LIKE AN EAGLE WHEN YOU HANG WITH TURKEYS.

> **SHARE YOUR GOALS WITH FRIENDS WHO WILL FORCE YOU TO LEVEL UP!**
> **(GO TO THE NEXT LEVEL)**

LEVEL UP!

PRINCIPLE 7:
SELECTIVELY SHARE YOUR GOALS WITH OTHERS

If you're going to stick to your goals and achieve them, you must be willing to SHARE YOUR GOALS with others like a *GOAL BUDDY*. Don't share your goals with those who are negative and will poo-poo (laugh at, be negative, or criticize) them. No, you want to share your goals with individuals who will:

1. Believe in you.
2. Encourage you.
3. Hold you accountable for achieving them.

Accountability and sharing your goals with others are essential to reaching them.

The (ASTD) American Society of Training and Development did a study and found out that you have a 65% chance of achieving your goals when you are accountable to someone.

The reason why you are more successful when you commit to sharing your goals with others is because, for the most part, you don't want to let them down, especially when the ones you are sharing your goals with are your parents, teachers, coaches, brother, sister or BFF (Best Friend Forever). In reality, you will happily buy your own excuses but wouldn't dare try to sell them to others. Being accountable and sharing your goals with others is to your advantage and will help you to achieve them.

What Is Accountability?
  -Being held responsible for the achievement of your goal.

Most youths today look at accountability as something negative however when you see it as a simple way of tracking your success so you can achieve your goals, it will improve your ability to achieve them tremendously. By far, ACCOUNTABILITY PRODUCES PROGRESS.

ACTION ITEM

Name at least FOUR people you can have as a *GOAL BUDDY* to share your goals with and hold you accountable to your goals.

PERSON #1
_____
_____
_____

PERSON #2
_____
_____
_____
_____

PERSON #3
_____
_____
_____
_____

PERSON #4
_____
_____
_____
_____

PRINCIPLE #7 MULTIPLE CHOICE

QUIZ

SHARING YOUR GOALS WILL HOLD YOU _____ TO YOUR GOALS.

A. STRONGLY

B. DAILY

B. ACCOUNTABLE

ACCORDING TO ATSD, YOU HAVE A 100% CHANCE OF ACHIEVING YOUR GOALS WHEN YOU ARE ACCOUNTABLE.

A TRUE

B FALSE

ACCOUNTABILITY ALWAYS PRODUCES _____.

A. PROGRESS

B. PLAY

C PURPOSE

D ALL THE ABOVE

SEE IT HAPPEN SO YOU CAN MAKE IT HAPPEN.

PRINCIPLE 8:
ADDING IMAGES TO YOUR GOALS

Adding and seeing images that match your goals will increase your motivation and desire to achieve them. Why? This is because our mind thinks in pictures, not in words. Also, images have a huge impact on our brains both consciously and subconsciously because they tell your mind what you want it to focus on. That's why vision boards are so powerful.

In case you are not knowledgeable about Vision Boards, a vision board is a visual representation of pictures, words, and images that describe the life of where you want to go, do, or become. Feeding your mind with these images brings you closer to achieving your dreams, goals, and destiny. The images on a vision board have a way of motivating and acting like magnets that will draw what you see toward you.

EXAMPLE:

I have on my vision board to attend the Olympics or meet an Olympian in the area of Track and Field. After the 2016 Olympics, for my birthday, my husband surprised me by having two Olympians Nia Ali, silver medalist, and Taylor Watson, gold medalist, (see above) show up at my birthday party celebration to wish me a "Happy Birthday." I believe my vision board, something that I view every day, drew them to me. The same thing can happen with your goals when you add images to them. A vision board is a perfect tool to utilize to keep your goals at the forefront of your mind.

PRINCIPLE #8 MULTIPLE CHOICE
QUIZ

ADDING IMAGES TO YOUR GOALS WILL DECREASE YOUR MOTIVATION TOWARDS THEM.

A. TRUE

B. FALSE

OUR MIND THINKS IN PICTURES AND NOT IN WORDS.

A. TRUE

B. FALSE

VISION BOARDS BRING YOU _____ TO ACHIEVING YOUR GOALS.

A. CLOSER

B. FARTHER

C. INSTANTLY

D. ALL THE ABOVE

ACTION ITEM

WRITE DOWN A LIST OF IMAGES, YOU WILL CUT OUT OR SEARCH THE WEB FOR, THAT MATCHES YOUR GOALS.

- [ ] _____
- [ ] _____
- [ ] _____
- [ ] _____
- [ ] _____
- [ ] _____
- [ ] _____
- [ ] _____
- [ ] _____
- [ ] _____
- [ ] _____

Answers

ANSWERS TO THE QUIZZES

- [ ] **WHY HAVE GOALS: PG.25**
  - C
  - A
  - D

- [ ] **PRINCIPLE #1: PG.33**
  - C
  - A
  - B

- [ ] **PRINCIPLE #2: PG.39**
  - A
  - A
  - B

- [ ] **PRINCIPLE #3: PG.48**
  - B
  - C
  - A

- [ ] **PRINCIPLE #4: PG.58**
  - B
  - B
  - A
  - B

- [ ] **PRINCIPLE #5: PG.62**
  - B
  - A
  - A

- [ ] **PRINCIPLE #6: PG.67**
  - C
  - A
  - C

- [ ] **PRINCIPLE #7: PG.73**
  - B
  - B
  - A

- [ ] **PRINCIPLE #8: PG.76**
  - B
  - A
  - A

SCORE _____

GIVE YOURSELF 5 POINTS FOR EACH CORRECT ANSWER
100+ ABOVE = EXCELLENT
90-99 = YOU DID GOOD
80-89 = YOU DID OKAY
79 OR BELOW = RETAKE THE ENTIRE TEST

CONGRATULATIONS!!!

You have successfully completed the *HAVE GUNS NOT GOALS ACTION GUIDE*, and therefore you are officially a part of the ELITE 8% Number.

To celebrate your accomplishment, place your name and date on the Achievement Certificate provided on the next page, print and frame it, and place it somewhere prominent to remind yourself of this great achievement and that you're now a part of the elite number...8%.

To produce a printable version of your Achievement Certificate or Daily Affirmations scan the QR code below or visit www.wandamartin.org.

SCAN QR CODE HERE

You did awesome!

CERTIFICATE
OF ACHIEVEMENT

PROUDLY PRESENTED TO:

_____

PRINT NAME HERE

This certificate certifies that the above name has successfully completed the **HAVE GOALS NOT GUNS** action guide course successfully and is now apart of the Elite Number 8%.

This certificate was awarded by:

Wanda Martin
Instructor, Author

_____

Date

Goal Setting Daily
AFFIRMATIONS

~I am a successful 8% Goal Achiever.

~Everything I touch turns into to gold.

~I accomplish all my goals daily, weekly & monthly.

~Failing only brings me closer to greatness.

~My goals are helping me to grow and be the best version of myself.

~I achieve everything I put my mind too.

~I have a special skill set as a youth/student/ that makes me unique, desirable and favorable.

~I will still win even if I am the underdog.

~My determination to win helps me achieve my goals.

~I am surrounded by positive and happy people who support me daily.

~I AM BLESSED~

THANK YOU!

I want to give a huge shout-out to my Heavenly Father for blessing me with the amazing opportunity to write this book.

A great big "Thank You" to my husband, Steve Martin for always going over and above to support me with all my goals and dreams and being in my corner every step of the way. Your love is truly extravagant.

To my two sons. Steven Jr. and Tony, mommy loves you, and truly thank you for allowing me to have the time to write this book without interruption. :)

To my sister, Alvita for your continued prayers.

Thank you to my church family, Higher Ground International for your continued prayers and support.

To Awinda, for all of your work and support to help me to see this project to the end. You are super amazing.

To Pastor Sharon Mcqueen for the many laughs that I needed to work through the challenges that I've faced when writing this book.

To Jack Canfield, Patty Aubery, James Malinchak, Deborah Smith Pegues, and Ms. Joyce Abbott...you all have inspired me in some amazing ways to complete this book, more than you'll ever know.

WWW.WANDAMARTIN.ORG

www.ingramcontent.com/pod-product-compliance
Lightning Source LLC
Chambersburg PA
CBHW082232180426
43200CB00037B/2840